TURN AND FACE THE WIND

Teresa Prins Wood

LUMINARE PRESS

WWW.LUMINAREPRESS.COM

Cover Concept by Teresa Prins Wood

Luminare Press
442 Charnelton St.
Eugene, OR 97401
www.luminarepress.com

ISBN: 978-1-64388-076-1
LCCN: 2019941769

TURN AND FACE THE WIND
is lovingly dedicated
to every grown-up child
orphaned late in life

Some of the poetry in this book
is presented without punctuation. This
traditional style of Native American
composition invites the reader to continue
in thought about what they've read.

TABLE OF CONTENTS

SOARING WITH THE WIND

I used to think it was an answer to prayer
some kind of blessing or a gift
to go through life
with the wind at my back
with the howling wind behind me
prodding me forward
occasionally with force
but most often
as a predictably steady breeze
I learned to move
with relative ease
through each chapter of my life
and then I got old
and then I got wise
and made the decision
to turn around
and face into the wind
and now that is how
I proceed through life
face to face with the storms
or the breezes
or whatever blows across my path
and it feels brave
and it feels right
I don't need to be escorted
nor shoved
nor guided toward my destination
with both feet firmly planted
the length of my back extended
my chin raised upward
I feel the cold
and kiss the world
as I dance into the wind

ABIDING

Let's build a house of love
where embraces
are always
within reach
where sleep
comes easy
inside strong walls
built on faith
in all that we believe
as true
where as we get older
each day
remains new
where tears
are never shed alone
where everyone
can come back home

TO WISDOM'S WARRIORS GO THE SPOILS

We had become like a feather in the wind
wishing that we had their money
so that we could purchase the land
and buy back our rights
and rebuild on the clay and the sand
that no one truly owns
We said When they throw their money
into the wind we must be there to gather it in
We must find a way to harness their storm
to somehow someday catch the wind

And so we watched And so we waited
until we knew what we must do
We wove our feathers together
and used them to harvest what they scattered
and in so doing we've won
We've finally won
By building sanctuaries lit brighter than the sun --
tunnels to catch the wind
into which they throw themselves and all they own
And we call the mighty conquest Casino

DEFENSIVE LINE

He had sharp edges
made sharper
across time
made sharper
by the dull friction
of an aggravated life
and so
when she came upon him
she didn't come too close
not so much in order
to protect herself
but rather
to avoid the possibility
of being accused
of being the one
who broke down
his defenses
she approached his world
with slow and steady
grace
with non judgmental
engagement
giving him the space he required
until he allowed

a closeness
that caused
her edges
(polished to softness
across time)
to be reflected
in the sharpness
of his being
and the softness
that defined her
eventually caused him
to lay his weapons down

PRISONER OF ACADEMIA

He said that over saturation
of any given thing
causes that entity
to diminish in value.
And then,
in case we didn't follow,
he attempted to clarify
his statement
by rewording just a bit
so that we would
better understand
that over exposure
or excessive involvement
with any given thing
lessens its worth.
He was the professor.
We were the students.
And so I wrote it down
and underneath
my lecture notes
I wrote:
Apparently
this lofty man
has never known true love.

MINING TOWN USA

Our skin was blue-ish grey
like ashes, like death
and we couldn't always catch our breath.
Some died so young
with never the chance
to go back and gather
the rest of their clan.
We thought we'd be mining
silver or gold
We mined iron ore and coal
and lived along the rail road tracks
in narrow little one-room shacks
called shotguns.
And the owner of the mine
was the owner the store.
Each Friday he paid us
as little as he could
only to take it all back
in trade for food.
A viscous cycle
of work
hunger
sleep
and the world was too dark
and the mines were too deep
and it hurt
when we breathed
in the freedom
of our new country

GYPSY VETERANS

"Move or die"
is the veteran's cry;
while those
who didn't serve
ask why.
The answer ~
as vivid,
as heated
as an ember:
"Whenever I sit still,
I am forced to remember."

LIMITED

We've cleverly figured out
how to light the sky
until it always looks like day;
and how to send our rockets
out to some galaxy
far, far away.

We've created piped-in music
so that it sounds
as if the trumpet and bassoon
are pounding out
a jazzy rhythm
right here in this room.

We've done all of this
and so much more,
yet we remain
without the cleverness
or the skill
to make Time stand still.

With all our wisdom
and all this power
that we so proudly hold,
still we wither
still we fade,
still we age to old.

LOVE, SOMETIMES

Like the roller coaster ride
along the midway
at the summer time county fair,
you can't get them to stop
just because
you're overcome with fear;
just because
you suddenly realize
that this whole thing is not fun.
And it's not like you can suddenly
break into a run --
You're buckled in, no turning back
and so you hold on tight
to survive until the ride is done.
And then, like a youngster
who escaped being caught
for disobeying some rule
you'd been diligently
taught to follow,
you thank God you're still alive,
get back in line
for another ride,
and plan to return
to the same thrilling terror
tomorrow.

REQUIEM

Amid the fury
and the blur
of fast paced living
You were
to me
the scenic route

CORONADO

We laughed that day
when the trolley
was headed our way
and we couldn't run fast enough
to get on board.

Over years
of wrongful accusations
and words not meant
to reach my ears,
the laceration
of a severed kinship
did not leave a scar.
It has remained forever
an open wound.

But we laughed that day
when the trolley
was headed our way
and we couldn't run fast enough
to get on board.

Whenever the memories
flood my mind
like storm waves
raging against the shore;

whenever the status
of our broken bond
stings my face
like a cold north wind,

I allow my mind
to turn back in time
to that day
when the sun was shining
and we were laughing
and the next trolley
was coming
to take us back home.

DANCING ONLY FOR EACH OTHER

His intoxicating laughter
pleases those around him
but she has heard the snorting
that resounds when they're alone.

Likewise, her ever buoyant smile
brings cheer to those around them
but he has wiped away her tears
for causes still unknown.

They twirl about to please the crowd
in this waltz of an existence
but in honesty of love's embrace,
they dance only for each other.

RESCUED

history can be
the events that haunt you
the guilt that taunts you
recalling mistakes
that won't go away
       history can be
       the pain you long to leave behind
       from wounds still bleeding
       incapable of healing
       in the past tense
history can be a trauma or
a reconstructed memory
where the details become
less demanding
more reasonable and kind
       history can be a mocker
       a lecher
       a cruel teacher
       demanding more
       than any one life can bear
but for those of us who've found the answer --
history becomes a foggy display
beneath a clear sky reminder
of all from which
we have been so mercifully
redeemed

MISSOURI BOYS

The boys who bale hay
at the end of the day
smell like onions;
like those big yellow onions
that sometimes burst open
on the ground
in my granddaddy's garden.

The boys who bale hay
at the end of each day
stand outside the corner store
drinking pop from green bottles
and their shirts are so wet
with the dust mixed in sweat
that sticks to their backsides like skin

and I'm wonderin'
if maybe the stink and the cling
is a strategic thing that God does
to keep the girls at bay ~~
to keep young girls far away
from the boys who bale hay,
from those beautiful boys of Summer.

CHRYSANTHEMUMS

The signature scent
of homecoming dances,
the chrysanthemum corsage
crushed beneath
an awkward teenage kiss.
And now each fall
I receive a fragrant call
from the garden
inviting me
to a high school homecoming
of the heart.

NECESSARY DISTRACTIONS

The smell of smoke
The heat of the sun
The sound
of someone crying
Distant thunder
The doorbell's ring
The growl of a dog
The chimes at noontime
Sirens close behind
A sudden downpour
A ringing telephone
That old time song
That certain shade of blue
The scent of magnolia
in mid-July
The memory of you.

CHILD OF THE PACIFIST

She required so very little of us.
"Play nice." That's what she said,
and, "Clean your plate"
and "Make your bed".
And "Pretty is as pretty does."
And so we thrived
in the bright sunlight
of a sheltering place
where there was never the need
to defend one's self
nor to feel inclined
to take a stand
against anything in particular,
that is, until we grew
and made our way
into the real world
where other folks
already knew
that you can't always
play nice,
and where it seemed
that everyone else
had come prepared
with weapons loaded,
ready to fight
in order
to merely survive.

WRECKLESS LOVE

first time out
no fear
no doubt
full speed ahead
nothing below
nothing above
with wild abandon
two innocents
without a clue
are traveling
at the speed of love

NY, NY

High rise stacks
of brick
and windows
that do, in fact,
scrape the sky
standing so tall
they block the sun
and beneath our feet
are concrete paths
made narrow by
incessant,
frantic movement
always heading
away from home;
rushing somewhere
in so distorted a world
that the honking
of a taxi's horn
or the big sigh
of city bus exhaust
is the morning music
to which
we're most
familiar.
This is the city:
to be so enclosed,
so surrounded,
and yet
so alone
that the coming on
at night
of the corner street light
is all that's left
to look forward to
in the city.

CARTERVILLE

Backyard mechanic? Heck no!
Out back's too hidden-way for me;
out front is where I aim to be,
where the massive, rusty old chain
and the fist-size hook
hang from the middle of the caterpillar tree.
Where the front porch swing is stacked high
with cables and belts, hoses and plugs,
screws I might need someday,
and a coil spring that
pretty much goes to nothing, but no,
I'm not about to throw any of it away.
You might say I've set up shop
under the catalpa tree
where passersby, at a glance can see
that here lives a real man --
a man of oil and grease and industry.
I'll not be found midafternoon
in some bar across town
with nothing to do but whine
about things I wish I'd done.
When the green bean-looking seed pods
dangle from this caterpillar tree,
look through the big leaves
and you just might find me

and if I'm not there,
then I know you know where
I'm most likely bound to be.
That soft wood bark
could never truly hold
the weight of the work
that these chains might claim
but the front yard
tells the whole world who I am,
or at least who I need for them to see.
God's truth is that I scoop up the caterpillars
(they're catalpa worms to me)
because they make good bait
and Center Creek is always there a waitin'
for worn-out, ole time
country fishin' boys like me.

LOST & FOUND

When our eyes met,
I had to look away.
I tried to avoid really looking at you
because I already knew
that it would take just one look
for me to get lost in your eyes.

Then suddenly I was captured
by the power of your smile
followed by your laughter,
filling my head with crazy dreams
of happily-ever-after.

I looked and, yes, it happened --
I got lost in those eyes
only to have you open wide the door
and welcome me in to
the center of your heart.

THE TREATISE

We didn't surrender
Refusing to go into battle
was our decision
based on love
We simply refused
to water this Earth
with the venomous blood
of those
who have no respect
for her worth
We were created to be
guardians of these grounds
believing
Earth need not be
the foundation
for the victory
of an unjust cause
And so we said
Take us if you must
but leave the magnificence
of our land
at peace

WHILE WAITING ON THE WARM

Together we'll wait out the winter
in shoes too tight
from doubled up socks
and sweatshirts that stay on
'til the end of the week.
We'll sit near the window
where the sun comes in best
and you'll read to me a biography
of someone who lived
a lifetime ago.
We'll eat popcorn for supper
and stay up late into the night
watching old movies in black and white
until the rhythm of your breathing
sings us to sleep.
We'll awaken to a morning
where frost's frozen fingers
have created a delicate masterpiece
on the front room window pane.
We'll flip a coin to see who'll go
for the paper and the mail,
and even if I lose the toss,
it's always you who'll bundle up
in coat, in hat, in gloves, and scarf,
layers of wool upon wool
enough to hike Pike's Peak
without a shiver
and I'll pray
that you don't slip-slide away
as together we conquer the winter
and wait upon the warm.

JANUARIES

Sometimes in the middle of winter
the sky will make an opening
as the clouds slide to the side
just a step or two
for the sun to appear
like a promise from heaven
that there's more of this to come

MY SISTER'S WEDDING

She had only just stopped being a child
and hadn't lived long enough
to be rebellious or wild.
She simply wanted someone to take her away
from all of the dysfunction.
She needed someone to look at her and say
"I'll take care of you."

Mother and Grandmother
said the dress will be blue
and nobody disagreed
because no one knew for sure
just exactly what to do.

I could sew and so it fell to me –
the task of making the dress.
They said, just something good for church,
nothing to impress;
not a gown to put away
for her own daughter's wedding
on some far-away day.

I should have said "No !"
"No, I will not make her dress
unless the fabric is ivory brocade,
trimmed in yards of ribbon and lace
with layers of sheer illusion to veil her face

and a bouquet of white roses and baby's breath
to hold in her trembling hands."

Then I could have watched with pride
as she said her vows in a gown of white
and became that young man's bride.
Then, no matter what the future held,
I'd have the memory of the way
that I became a rebel for my sister's wedding day.

If I could do it over, I would.

THINK ABOUT IT

To commit oneself
to being a person
who
loves mercy
involves more
than a willingness
to forgive.
To love mercy
also means
to *act upon*
each opportunity
to be
forgiving.

BETWEEN THIRD AND HOME

From the batter's box,
it all starts out
looking as if every base
is separated by a million miles
or at least fifty years,
and so you take each one
at a pace most reasonable
for the you you know yourself to be.
And, unlike friends long gone,
you don't steal away
hurrying toward home,
rushing onward to see what's next.
And by the time you've learned the rules
and see that there are no do-overs,
no lemme start agains --
you slow your roll
and savor your time
in the field.
And when it all starts moving
way too fast
and you find yourself
on third at last
and you know
you've not much further to go,
you gather your wits
and say to yourself,
Although the outcome
will be grand,
I'll not be stealing home.

THE MARRIAGE POLITIC

I'm not saying that there should be term limits,
I'm just saying that there should be terms
so that at the end of a certain number of years,
one would be required
to campaign for the attention,
for the devotion,
for the continuation
of all that made up the previous
span of time.
I believe these terms,
if taken to heart,
might inspire the mundane,
motivate self improvement,
boost the economy,
and remind us how to love again.

SOMETIMES THAT ONE SONG

The notes
float
above your head
not like medicine injected
but like medicine
absorbed
when one opens the pores
of one's pain
and allows the sound
entrance
into the brain
into the place
where memories lodge
where sentiment
is stored
where comfort
is awakened
where
I'm going to be alright
becomes a thought
then forms
into a sentence
and then into
a logical notion
into a belief
into a resounding
auditory potion
into true healing
Music is medicine

HOWLING AT THE MOON

Once
in the pit
of deepest despair
I pledged my allegiance
to the moon
and then
when my heart
had made its repair
I realized
I'd pledged too soon
And now
every time
he comes out to shine
with the fullness
of his old bald head
winking at me and
wearing that grin
I find myself beside myself
suddenly locking eyes
with him
I want to howl
and howl
and howl
Ah proof once again
that the wild wolf
within us
remains bound
and then determined
to set itself free
now and then

IMPRISONMENT SELF IMPOSED

Among those of us
born into freedom
are the many
who grow up to spend
the next
seventy or so years
enslaving themselves
through
luxuries
rituals
and obsessions
of their own choosing
all of which
in short time
join together
to form a prison
without those
born into freedom
ever recognizing
that they've locked
themselves behind
unrelenting
unescapable
gilded bars
of their own design

NINE TENTHS OF THE LAW

It was not ignorance on our part
we were not stupid nor naive
and although they did not speak
our native tongue
we knew what they were saying
> They wanted us to give to them
> something that we did not own
> They wanted us to surrender
> something that we'd always known
> was never ours to begin with
We had been entrusted
to live on this land
to love and to nurture
all that the Earth put forth
to be her devoted caretakers
> and so we did
> with gratefulness of spirit
> and humility of heart
> and the very best of ourselves
> with a willingness to share
while never intending
to release our strong hold
on the land that gave us life
We were not ignorant nor stupid
we were neither foolish nor naive
> The strong barrier between us was their notion
> that we were somehow in a position
> to fulfill their demand to own this land –
> this precious entity
> beyond the scope of true possession

NEAR THE SHIPYARD

On Puget Sound
the sea gulls see it all
but never tell a soul
where the body might be found;
because when lovers
go their separate ways,
sometimes the memories
end up drowned
in the murky darkness
off Puget Sound
were salt and fresh water merge.
It has happened so often
that the gulls no longer care
when someone, broken hearted,
stands there
looking at the water
as if therein exists
the contents of their history
or the only solace
to remove the pain.

MORE ABOUT MAGNOLIA
(and in support of older girls)

If you are determined
to choose
a sapling or,
even more extreme,
to plant one from seed,
keep in mind
that she's going to take
a long, long time
to bloom.
Her full flower
won't set on
until year fifteen.
Oh yes, she'll be evergreen
and you'll be waiting
for anything
that resembles maturity.

So reconsider, if you will,
the older magnolia
who's been around
harsh winds
and the hottest
southern ground;
who's trunk is thicker
and more tolerant of cold.
Choose her –
she's not brand new
but she's certainly not too old.
Take her home, make her yours
and you will wonder
why you waited so long.

WOUNDED

Broken crayons
color just as brightly,
just as clearly,
just as rightly,
as when they
stood tall
in the safety
of their little boxes.
Peeled away,
broken,
crushed under foot,
it may be a bit
more difficult
to work their magic,
but with courage,
broken crayons will
create a masterpiece
so admired
that onlookers
stand in awe;
and with regard to
the condition of the
instrument used,
they are never the wiser.

REALITY CHECK

When old age
mockingly dares to say,
"The greatest of my
accomplishments
are all behind me now;
the best I had to offer
exists far in the past.",
Maturity
sarcastically replies,
"Well, I've found
that I'm okay with that."
Wisdom agrees
and says with a smile,
"So come on,
let's sit back,
relax awhile,
and take the time
to truly find
that sense of satisfaction
in the good
that has been done;
all the while
casting our gaze
on the joy
that is to come
as a result
of living well."

IT'S A SOUTHERN THANG

Southwest Missouri Ozarks ~~
Where "bring a meat dish"
means fried chicken.
The meaning of
"bring a vegetable",
there are two:
A big bowl of potato salad
or some brown sugar
barbeque beans with bacon,
either one will more than do.

Southwest Missouri Ozarks ~~
Where friendship is extended
in the warmth of a tater-tot casserole.
Love is culinarily expressed
with a deep dish home-made pie;
and if they show up at your door
with both,
somebody must be out of this world
or someone's about to
lay down an' die.

NEVER LOOKING BACK

Her life was filled
with sudden endings
without the benefit
of goodbye
and so she adjusted
her sails accordingly
and learned to live
as if every encounter
might be the last
and each port of call
would exist in memory
once she drifted in departure
from the safety of the harbor
enthusiastically full throttle
out into new waters

LOVE ME WITH MY SHOES ON

When I'm bundled up
in layers of sweaters, scarves,
and itchy socks inside of boots
ready to step out into winter;

or when there's dirt
under my fingernails
and I've been kneeling
on damp soil, planting spring bulbs;

when I'm stinky with sweat
from summertime's heat,
don't love me less
if I'm not at my best.

Love me when I'm bulky.
Love me dirty.
Love me hot.
Always love me more, not less;

and I will fall for you anew
each and every time you do.

THE POLITICS OF LIES

Lies
are the mortar
that build
the stone walls
that divide
and then
separate
our hearts
from exploring
our potential
to love

JUST MINDNG HIS OWN

Down in southern Colorado,
out in Pueblo to the east,
where the mountains enclose the valley
like a broadcast studio,
like someplace that is the opposite
of a private confessional,
Mason will stand at the edge of his land
and listen as the wind
blows the life of his neighbors
out of their old barn and into his fields.
Sometimes it sounds to Mason
like somebody is yelling
and sometimes there is cursing,
a sudden sound of smacking
with the pounding of a fist against a wall,
and the wailing of a baby,
and then there's total silence.
Minutes later, there'll be laughter
and the blaring of a radio;
and he hears two voices singing
loud and upbeat or smooth and slow
and he figures that thcy're dancing
and probably having a ball.
And so when it seems to Mason
as if nothing else will happen,
he goes back to the plowing
of the soil in his own field.

CONFESSIONS CULINARY

The reviews call her work lavish,
opulent, full-bodied like good wine.
One described it as a delicious read;
another said that at page 101
he could almost taste
the salty ocean water on his tongue.
She wonders if they have uncovered
her methodology
(which she meticulously tries to hide).
She is an artist
fueled by carbohydrates.
Her best work has been done
under the influence
of angel hair pasta, un-plated.

I'M GOOD

Don't dramatically give up
your place in line
Don't flamboyantly surrender
this space in time
Don't theatrically nod at me
just to be kind
I 've neither the energy
nor the state of mind
for your outward demonstrations
of charity
The memory of one
genuine act of compassion
or kindness or love
even something as simple
as a smile
has the purity of power
to carry me through
for quite a long long while

LAMENT OF THE BIBLIOPHILE

The final page,
those last few words,
for me, it's never easy.
Regardless of how it comes to a close,
I'm never ready;
I don't want to go.
Between the lines, the words are saying,
"That's all. We're done. Move on."
But it's not that simple for me.
I read and I become one with the story.
I hold as tight to the edge of the boat
in the dark of night on that stormy sea in chapter three,
as do the weary mariners
who've become my travel companions.
I dance along with smiling strangers
at the spring-fest celebration in the park.
I sit under the shade of the umbrella at the tiny cafe
and watch as summertime people walk by.
I cry when the sister dies
after a seemingly endless struggle
that gave her family and myself
those restless, dreamless nights.
And then it ends.
Like saying goodbye to dear friends,
you close a book
that's been open for so long,
and suddenly they're gone …
and I have to find someone new to love
and I have to learn to move on;
and I'll continue grieving just a bit
until, with a surge of new life, I open the next book.

INTO THE GREAT BEYOND

All of us are pilgrims
making our way home.
Some of us walk along side of a friend
while some of us journey alone.
Some of us walk with a caravan
amidst the laughter and songs of the crowd,
while others choose a divergent path
where the noise of fellow pilgrims
is muffled and less loud.
Some chose a road of solitude,
accompanied by memories
of a long-time-ago day
when the road that leads us homeward
                            seemed
                    so very
                            much
                                farther
                                    away.

MOON RIVER

At an old time shop
in a far away town
crackling static blared
from a tiny worn out radio
until the shopkeeper
antique as his surroundings
turned the dial
and began to smile
as the song came on
Then you smiled too
and took my hand
and danced me around
the creaking hardwood floor
in a musical embrace
along the aisle between
the newsstand magazines
and the souvenirs

LEGENDARY MOTHER

He marched onto the battlefield
leaving behind his Mother
his younger brother
a precious bride
and a newborn child
He went out to fight against
what is cruel
what is evil
what is treacherous
and unjustly wild
On his return
still walking strong
he learned that his mother
was dead and gone
Exercising the powerful force
of maternal love
she had stared directly
into the face of the sun
and saw what lie ahead
That at the end
of summer's season
many a brave warrior
would be dead
But not her son
because Heaven heard her
as she pled
Here I am
take me instead

ANTIQUE LOVE

Their house is on the corner
at the four-way stop
and every morning I'd see them
sitting on their front porch swing.

They were two old souls never speaking,
never moving;
both looking in opposite directions
every day on my way to where I was going.

And I'd think:
Yep, this must be how it is
after too many years together --
Nothing left to say, nothing left to do,

both probably thinking identical thoughts
and nothing's ever fresh, nothing's ever new.
Then one morning I was half an hour late
to the four-way stop.

I saw them walking across the yard.
His arm was around her shoulder,
her arm around his waist,
and when they stopped,

she looked upward to his face
and they both appeared to be laughing
as he planted several kisses
on the top of her head.

And I thought as I drove away,
Yes, yes, yes! I want it to be
exactly like that
for me someday.

POST TRAUMATIC

O constant warrior
making everywhere you walk
your battleground
Thirsty for victory
Hungry for the sound
of destruction
when you take another down
with your words
with your very essence
with the pretense of dominance
in the presence of weakness
and surrender
Did no one ever teach you
or did you learn
and then forget
how to live in peace?

UNEXPECTED ENCOUNTER

When put upon by mercy
my spirit called to memory
the contract I'd made
with myself
to put the past behind.
So silently I placed a prayer
at the forefront of my mind
asking that somehow
you had done the same
but that if selective memory
still remained your game
you'd find a way
to remember a day
when while in
each other's presence
we smiled.

MY OFFERING

Let me give you
a heart
to beat in time with yours,
good coffee
in the morning,
a hand that you can hold,
ideas
creative and ever new,
two feet
to walk along with you,
a place
you'll want to return to,
long legs
that keep you looking,
a future
better than your past,
warm nights
of passion or of rest,
a spacious place
with room for two.
I want to give my love to you.

EXPLAINING DEATH

Take into your hand a stone
and throw it far across the water.
As you stand on the shoreline
watching it sail,
watching it spin
until it skips and splashes
and then suddenly sinks,
do you perceive
that the stone is gone
or do you reason
that it is merely out of
your range of vision?
The stone didn't cease to be.
It now resides in a deeper place
where, from here along the shore,
it seems long gone,
but, in truth,
the stone lives on,
remaining as vital,
although elsewhere present,
as you and me.

IDENTITY SEARCH

Go ahead and lose yourself
in something or someone.
Here's a one-time pass
to surrender your identity,
to say goodbye to the real you
by clothing yourself
in the overly heavy amour of a warrior
or an ill-fitting garment of a lover
or the wolfish sheep skin of an enabler
or the straight jacket
of an occupational over achiever
to briefly become the someone
you were never intended to be.
In so doing you will hopefully
learn two important lessons,
one being that the road back home
is traveled alone,
is all uphill, and hard to climb
And lesson number two
is that the journey back
is worth the struggle
if during your travels
you come to discover
how to live in love with the truth
of the authentic you.

WHINE & CHEESE

It's poetry, for Pete's sake ~
It's not an editorial piece
or a statement of faith
or a work of fiction
or an autobiography.
It's just poetry!

Whoa. Wait (Uh oh).
On second thought,

It's poetry ~
a personally relevant
editorial piece,
sometimes a statement of faith,
occasionally fictional,
frequently autobiographical,
and more, so very much more.

Whew ~ I'm glad
we got that straightened out.

OLD HIGHWAY 82

Along the Arkansas-Mississippi line
where the roadways are framed
by wild magnolia
cypress and pine
a kaleidoscope of greens
that hypnotize the eyes
until I could lose my mind
just thinking about you
and wishing you were here
near the Southeast Arkansas border
where the bayous pull you
into Mississippi
where the Chicot
and waters to the north
feed thirsty cotton fields
to the south
and everything is fertile
I want to sit beside you
on the grassy slope
along the bayou just west
of the thorny mayhaw trees
near summer sweet raspberries
growing along the footpath
that leads straight
into the cool waters
of the muddy Mississippi

SUMMER'S LAST SONG

Cooler nights set the stage
for spectacular days;
re-energized displays
of breathtaking beauty
in summer's final act.
Powerful, like an encore
before September
dims the lights
and throws open the door
to autumn.

SOLO TU   *

I will never fall in love
with you again
and that is a very,
very good thing.
When I first fell for you,
I fell so hard
and so deep
that once I got back
onto my feet
and saw just what I'd done,
I said,
This is where I want to stay --
in love, beside you every day;
I will never fall like that again.
No need to.
I plan to spend my whole life
on this sweet ground,
precisely where I fell;
where you helped me up,
where I stand today,
where you stand beside me,
where I can honestly say
that I'll never fall in love again.
And that, my dear,
is a very good thing ~
To live in love
without fear
of falling.

* Solo tu is the Spanish version of 'only you'

DAY OF RECKONING

Here is how you will know
when you've finally
gotten too old :
When,
in watching them
come and go,
there is
no easy season
awaiting you,
no better days
to look forward to.
Tell yourself today
that *that* day
will never come.
LIVE
believing
in tomorrows.

PLEASE. PLEASE. PLEASE.

How do you
restrain your weapon?
How do you
look evil in the eye?
With pity
in knowing
that every boy
has a mother
who does not
want her son
to die.

CHAMPIONS

Naked.
Stripped bare
by yet another winter,
the trees without their leaves
invite us all to see
what it's like to be fragile.
 Take time to look closely.
 The lesson
 of the skeleton of the tree
 is that
 when stripped to bare,
 down to the bone,
when what we thought to be loveliest
appears to be long gone,
removed by what is harsh,
and what is cold,
and what is dark,
 what remains
 is that which makes one strong
 and that which causes one to stand.
 What remains
 is that to which
 one's roots are bound.

LIKE IT WAS YESTERDAY

The world stopped turning
and traffic stopped moving
Horns stopped honking
as music stopped playing
People stopped breathing
and the wind stopped stirring
No one was being born
No one had just died
The air was still
neither warm nor cold
and the only thing he saw
was her eyes
her mouth
her face
her being
And the only thing he heard
was the pounding of his heart
as she reached to take his hand
And the only thing he felt
was the strong magnetic field
drawing them nearer
one to the other
And nothing else mattered
at that moment in time

THE ANCHOR

At night I set sail far, far from the shore
en route to calm waters so crystalline
that my eyes see clearly
what lies beneath the deepest of the deep.
And while the body is asleep,
the mind explores new worlds.
But regardless of the adventures
and discoveries in my dreams,
when morning comes,
I ride the tide
back to the shoreline that awaits me
where it is imperative that I drop anchor
before setting foot on the hard ground
of reality.
The anchor is balanced and weighty
to secure the contents of the day,
whether wondrous, whether rough.
Shore duty is a beautiful life
made easier by the fact
that my anchor is Almighty God.

INDIVISIBLE

The downside of being a warrior
is the inability to remove the armor
when the battle is finally over
or while walking through
a valley of peace
The refusal to lay the weapons down
when it's time to rest at the end of the day
The private denial and disbelief
when a battle is won
Failing to report Osiquu*
when it's finally time to go home
and worse of all infractions
the tendency to forget
that you did not fight alone

* Osiquu is a common Cherokee word
  used to declare that all is well

BARGAINING CHIP

All that I'll require
in this adventure called life
is that half of the time
you let me drive

OKINAWA

Stay with me
stay
until day break
and then go
while I'm sleeping
go
in the same way
that I would leave you
if I was a sailor boy
learning the lessons
of war
on a faraway shore
with a shipload
of brothers
to return to
and so he left her
in the darkness
of springtime
alone
with the scent
of cherry blossoms
and he left her
with a child
who came after
the ship had sailed
a baby boy whose eyes
were her forever reminder
of the one and only time
she ever pleaded
with a man
of the one and only time
she would ever again
beg someone
to stay

UNCONDITIONAL

Do you have a thinking mind,
a beating heart,
long arms on either side
with fingered hands
at both their ends?
Well then,
I can't see any reason
for us to not be friends.
Does a vast expanse of flesh
and a collection of hard bone
make up the container
that is your body,
the carriage that is your home?
Well then,
there simply is no cause
to not call you friend.
The things that you are bound to do,
the places that you'll go,
life choices you prefer,
the you I'll come to know ~
While those things attempt to separate
this bond that I'll defend,
I intend to think of you
for always as my friend.

PLEASING THE PALATE

One small taste
of something sweet
before I die.
My grandmother
would say that
after she would eat.
She'd request
just one small taste
of something sweet;
and that's how I came
to do the same.
Needing something sweet
before I die,
craving something good ~
not only at the table,
and not merely with food.

TAKE COURAGE

What if someone you knew
took hold of your hands
and said,
Together, we'll get through this.

What if that someone reminded you
that there is nothing
you can't do ~ saying,
You're going to be just fine;

take it easy, give yourself time.
You'll never be alone,
and if you get lost,
I know the way home.

What if someone who cares
said those words to you,
what would you do?
Alright then my friend,
believe and consider it done.

HEART OF THE STORM

He told her, I've been known to be
a hurricane without warning
forming at most anytime of year.
She said, Then I will be your sea wall.
When he said, My torrents have been known
to tear at the shoreline, leaving destruction
and desolation behind,
she said nothing
because she understood his truth.
And so the years passed
and the tides changed.
The sun rose every morning
and then set to rise again
without so much as threat of storm,
without so much as crashing waves.
The storms never came
simply because he knew
that their potential for ruin
was weakened
the stronger their love-bond grew.
They lived their life together,
smooth sailing in calm waters
where the only uncontrollable
force of nature
was their passion for each other
and her look that dared him
to allow her to calm the storm.

IGOHIDA   *

Your Sovereign
is the arrow
that pierces
the darkness
Your faith
is the quiver
that holds
the arrow close
Your obedience
gives you strength
to march forward
to the battle
Your devotion
reminds you
that victory awaits

* The Cherokee word for Everlasting is Igohida

SMILE WHEN YOU SAY THAT

Right this moment I'd like it to be
that my super-power is to be able
to actively enforce the phrase
"If you keep making that face,
you're going to stay that way."
Ha! That'd teach 'em a thing or two.

But privately, between me and you,
how about if my super-power
was to make it so that
every fast food sandwich
was served exactly as it appears
on the advertisement.

Okay, here's my truth:
My super-power, if I could make it so,
would be that everyone went to bed at night
with a belly full of healthy food
and a beautiful, peaceful smile on their face
that would always have cause to stay that way.

WHAT'S IN A NAME

He's probably still around,
this guy I sort of knew in 1982,
who named his first born daughter Chevelle
and his second girl was Nova.
I imagine he'd love to have had a son
to call Malibu or Monza,
but nope; daughter number three was Caprice.
I never asked, but I suspect
that he came from a school of thought
or a tribal practice, or vehicular religion
whose followers bestow upon their offspring
the title of some thing they love
enough to savor the sound of its name every day
and throughout long nights and lullabies
for a full eighteen to twenty years.
I'm glad I was not aware
of that approach to naming a child.
In fact, were they privy to the method,
I'm certain that my own children
would be grateful beyond measure
that at the time of their birth I did not employ
the name-what-you-adore technique.
I look at family photographs,
I think of Christmas cards,
of singing "Happy Birthday"
and cannot imagine including the words
(that is to say, the names)
Pasta   and   Sleep.

PRELUDE

If you ever find
that you have
a lifetime
to spare,
I'd love to share
every minute of it
with you.

SOFT

Soft
falling snow
light rain
warm sand
beneath bare feet
moonlight filtered by
a cloudy sky
the scent of hyacinths
on a springtime breeze
the color of morning glories
and sweet peas
a whisper of the wind
through willow trees
tears of gratitude that
drop you to your knees
Soft is all of these
and more
In the midst of the harshness
of everyday life
somehow these things
remain
soft
to remind us
that eventually
better days
will come

JUSTICE

For some,
it's a very long journey.
Don't measure their progress
with your own time clock.

CHOCOLATE

Full of sweetness but bad for the blood.
Full of calories and bad for the body.
Full of guilt, thus bad for the mind;
but I want some every day.
I want it when I celebrate
or when I am in pain.
I want it because it energizes.
Smooth and sweet or dark and bitter,
it doesn't matter.
It pleases so deliciously,
all the while destroying me;
tainting my blood, messing my mind,
filling me with delight,
then shaming mercilessly.
Captivating all my senses,
leaving me wanting more.
I want it and I want it now,
toying with me,
wrecking me,
leaving me satisfied and guilty
and wrong all combined.
Still, I crave it just the same,
this undisciplined indulgence
that can make the world go away
until nothing exists
but the fullness of the pleasure
of sweet chocolate.
You, dear man,
were my chocolate.

AZURE INCROYABLE   *

In the city of Nice,
in the country of France,
we'd planned to go
to the Promenade,
to the palais,
and then to the museum.
But I said,
Go along without me,
I'm staying here on le prom.
I'm going to sit here at this table
in this open air café
and look at the incredible blue
winter sky
until something
that would dare to compare
to its beauty
passes by
or until I die,
whichever comes first.

* 'Azure Incroyable' is a way of describing
  an incredible blue sky in French

IDENTITY CRISIS
And the Pitiful Abuse of Power

No one ever taught her
how to say no
and so when she finally said it
and this big, wide world
didn't catastrophically
come to an explosive end,
and she didn't grow horns
or warts on her skin,
she decided to say it again
and again
and again.
She said, "No"
and was immediately amazed
at the self-satisfying power
available in so small a word;
no,
No.
NO!
And that is how she unintentionally
went spiraling downward
into an apathetic, passionless world
where no one knows her anymore;
and where she no longer
recognizes herself.

DANGEROUS   DEVOTION

Please don't engage in a life
whereby your happiness
depends entirely upon
your children.
Doing so creates for them
a responsibility too weighty
for anyone
at any age
to imagine themselves
able to bear.

FRIEND OF THE ATHIEST

She found herself quite liberal in her tolerance of others,
in her willingness to accept those unlike herself.
She thought herself diverse and unafraid
of blatant differences that attempt to set her apart
from those whose way of living
bears no resemblance to her own.
She refused to separate based solely on disparities;
choosing instead, to embrace those things
that make each one of us unique.
That is, until the day she listened to him say
that eternity is a fallacy,
that he did not believe in the existence
of a being greater than himself,
that he refused to accept the concept of Creator
or that of an ever-present Power.
She saw that he did not flinch nor appear undecided,
or willing to consider alternatives to his belief.
On hearing his declaration,
she felt as if she'd been walking
along a familiar pathway
only to discover herself on an unfamiliar road
where in the dust sat a starving man
unwilling to be fed.

THE AFTERTASTE OF REALITY

It's just that on occasion
more frequently of late
there's something wrong with my coffee
there's a bitterness to the taste
and the cream seems not as sweet
I've got to rectify the situation
and I've got to do it soon
and I'm fairly certain
that what this means
is that I'll not be
looking at the paper
or turning on
the morning news
until after my body
and my mind
have fully absorbed
the benefits
of two strong cups
of my daily brew.

HOSPICE

He told her,
Once I get there
I'll be fine.
My body's worn
and I've grown old,
but I've prepared
for this time
in my heart
and in my mind;
I just wish that somebody
could come
and walk me home
because I've never been one
who cared much
for traveling on my own.

ADIOS

When someone dies,
let's not say
Goodbye
or So long.
Let's have no more
Farewells or
I'll see you later.
Au revoir
slides beautifully
off of the tongue,
but that goodbye
would imply
that you expect
the departed to return.
When someone dies,
let's accept our loss
by expressing our truth ~
Let's always and only say
Adios.
A Dios.
Go to God.

DO NOT PASS GO

She thought life was like
some sunny day
midway into spring
where you go outside
to the garden
and throw out
everything
you've grown tired of
and then plant
what satisfies you now,
never realizing
that down deep in the soil
beneath her feet
were the remains of things
long forgotten,
roots that still grew deep
and remnants of every
seed she'd ever sown.

HYMN

You are the words to every verse I ever learned
You are the meaning to every song I've ever loved
You are the harmony to every melody I've heard
You are the definition of music to me

ORDER UP

I'll take life
with a side
of love

SO JUST BEAT IT

Oh dear !
It would appear
that I have
screwed up yet again
in my attempt to win
you for my own.

Please erase
from your mind
my strange
dim-witted
and clearly blind
approach to romance.

Never again
will I ask
you to dance
until I've heard
at least one full stanza
of the song being played !

In desperation
and using my best voice
I'd suggested that
it was time for us to dance.
And then, Oh no!
What a mood killer
when the song that boomed
into the room
was the full length version of Thriller.

TOUGH LOVE

I make no claim
to psychic powers
but a good measure
of intuition
is enough
to have assured me
that you, my friend,
are traversing
an unfamiliar road;
unlit, unkempt,
unrighteous,
unwise.
Let it come as no surprise
when I do not stoop
to help you up
once you fall
and find yourself exposed.
I'll be here waiting
once you take a stand
but until then,
you're on your own.
Or let me say it differently ~
you're sailing on a troubled sea
and sometimes
the course to recovery
must be sailed on a ship
alone.

RECONCILLIATION

The most challenging aspect
in learning to love
your enemy
is coming to
that place in time
when you discover
that it is necessary
to quit hating
yourself.
Once you make peace
and finally forgive,
you will have
granted yourself the right
to truly begin to live.

BELONGING

Once upon a time
not so long ago
the words
you belong to me
were not sexist
patriarchal
chauvinistic
or wrong
The words meant
I will love
and protect you
through life's storms
in times of war
and even more so
in times of peace
when the silence of
the unknown
troubles your soul
The words meant
that your life
is of more value
to me
than my very own
Once upon a time
not many years ago
to possess another's heart
did not equate
to dominance or control
I remember it like yesterday
because I too
once gave my heart away
when I belonged
to you.

REVIVED

When you rolled the stone
away from my heart,
you let escape all bitterness and hate;
you let escape self doubt and blame,
regrets and confusion, guilt and shame --
all of which held the stone in place,
a stone that could not be moved
by the power or the love
of anyone but You.

THE PRICE OF BITTERNESS

How long can you hold
a grudge?
For less than a split-second
(if that long).
Thereafter, the grudge
holds you
in a heavy, weighted, dark,
strangulating embrace;
in a clenching grip
that holds you back,
slows you down,
and fixes your focus
on the past
rather than on your future.

FIDELITY

Don't ask her for a late night promise
when she's in need of sleep
or when she's only just awakened
and not yet had her coffee.
Don't ask her to take a vow
if the moon is new, or full, or waning.

It's not that she's a promise breaker.

It's more that she is so bound to keep her word,
that she'll do so regardless of whether or not
she is suited to the challenge.
She'll keep her word and remain true
long after the promise breakers
like you
are gone.

EVERY NOW AND THEN

In response
to the foul events
of this day
I am seriously
considering
engaging in
an ocular flush;
a cleansing
to detoxify
each eye.
Translation:
I feel like
I am just about
to allow myself
another
good cry.

WHEN WITH BEST INTENTIONS

Enabling
is that act of love,
that smooth and soothing balm
that greases the tracks
to hold them back
from moving forward
on their own.

ENGULFED

Let's swim out to the edge of forever
Let's get lost
in the sound of the waves
Let's stand in the sand
with you holding my hand
and we'll pretend
that the ocean floor
is pulling us away
from the crowd
on the shore
Let's allow the surge of this tide
to bind us together
while we stand side by side
as children of the sun
nvda diniyoli *

* Cherokee expression for
'children of the sun' or 'sun's children'

PRISONER IN THE BIG HOUSE

He looks out at the ocean
as he sits between marbled columns
on his Pacific-facing Grecian-styled west balcony.
He's comfortable in his Italian leather
high back swivel chair,
enjoying imported Columbian coffee
with a splash of Irish crème
while smoking a Cuban cigar.
His cook, who's from Honduras,
sets French toast and scrambled eggs
topped with Swiss cheese
onto the Danish-made coffee table
just to the left of his knees that are covered
with an Egyptian cotton throw.
She pours into a fine-China cup
his English tea at three
and evening meals of Polish sausage
rolled into flaky empanada dough
with a side of cold gazpacho
and a shot of scotch is the way
he tends to prefer to end each day.
And he's been to all those countries
and he's slept in all those beds
but still in all the memory
that will not escape his head
is of the simplicity and tenderness
that was his a lifetime ago;
when he and his siblings crowded together
under the warmth of a worn out quilt
in a squeaky wrought iron bed
in the corner of a shanty that was home
where the measure of wealth was love
and the world was truly his own.

HIBERNATION

I wonder
which passes
the quickest --
Is it three months
or twelve weeks?
Which is easier to endure,
one polar season
or eighty-four days?
Come rest here beside me,
warm your body
under covers
next to mine.
Together
we will weather
another winter
and share our dreams
of summertime.

TU ERES MI SOL   *

Against the warped wood
window pane
I stand listening
to the rain
thinking once again
about when we
were insane enough
to believe that
summer and youth
like trust and love
would last forever.

* Tu eres mi sol translates from
Spanish to English as You are my sun

UNREASONABLE DEMANDS

Be my umbrella.
Cover me,
cloak me
in an open-ended embrace,
exposing yourself
in order to protect me
from things that I probably
ought to endure on my own.
I won't need you every day
but sometimes I'll want you
towering over me,
shielding me from life's storms;
keeping me dry
and keeping me warm
and helping me
to look as good in the end
as I did in the beginning
of each blustery storm.
I want to be able to put you away,
always knowing where you are
in case I need
to be near you again;
keeping you sometimes out of sight,
but always close at hand.
O, man! What am I saying?
God forbid that anyone
would ever require
that kind of devotion
from the likes of me.

IN THE DEAD OF WINTER

Lord give me
darkness
and give me
light
to recognize
the wrong
to choose
the right
to live
the day
and love
the night
Give me
the cold winds
and then
soft rains
I'll enjoy
the comfort
and endure
the pain
in the darkness
of winter
until the sun
shines again
But mostly
please
give to me
that precious sense
of calm

THE ART OF PERSEVERANCE

Sometimes
you've gotta stand up straight
thinking like an eagle
gather your coat around you
pretending it has wings
hold it tightly to your chest
like a mighty warrior's shield
then lift your face up skyward
and sail into the wind

And if the wind is so rough
that it knocks you to the ground
get yourself back up again
by thinking like an eagle
pretending you have wings
holding fast to your warrior's shield
you have the courage
you have the strength
to win the day one breath at a time

REALISTICALLY SPEAKING

Yes
I come with scars
But please know
that it is not
your responsibility
to make them disappear
Your job is to simply
make me forget
that they are even here

FOUND

Growing up, she was strongly warned
to not ever become vain
and so she learned to never lock eyes
with her reflection in a mirror.

Not wanting to be self-centered,
she disciplined her mind
to never think of herself until
she had first thought of others.

A diagnosis of Egotistic or Narcissistic
was something she'd nervously avoid
when in the presence of strangers, coworkers,
and those near and dearest to her heart.

Never wanting to flaunt an impressive education,
she kept her thoughts, her knowledge,
and the very best of her intentions to herself;
choosing instead to vote with the crowd.

Until one day upon waking
and walking to the sink
where she washed from her eyes
the sand of yet another dreamless sleep,

she glanced up into the mirror
and was startled and then surprised
to see the face of a woman
whom she hardly recognized.

Somewhat resembling her mother,
except that what she saw
was vibrant and soft
and strangely beautiful.

Who is that? She wondered
as she walked to the telephone
to call in to work to say
that she'd be staying home today.

Then going back to the mirror,
she spoke to her reflection,
boldly proclaiming,
Good Morning and Hello !

You, young lady,
are someone
I'm about to get to know,
starting right now.

ELBOW ROOM

I could sit with you forever,
just talking, drinking tea,
and laughing away the day.
I could share a million meals with you
and never grow tired
of taking notice of the odd taste
among the fashionistas
or the day-old bread.

I wouldn't hesitate
to accept your invitation
to travel around the globe
a time or two –
to watch the sunrise
in Aberdeen
or the rain in Barcelona,
just me and you.

But at the end of the day
I want to be alone.
I want to walk
my own self home.
I need that time and space
and sense of place
in order to be good
at being with another.

So, if that's something
you can understand,
then hold tightly
to this heart
that I'm placing in your hand
and say you'll
come around again
tomorrow.

ALL IN THE MIND

He hated himself for not telling her
the things he wanted to say.
He wrote them all down
in a love letter
but then crumpled it up
and threw it away.
It read:
You are perfection
in the midst of chaos.
Your eyes are a fire
that ignites my soul.
Your smile
turns every fear I have
from brokenness
into becoming whole.
Well, maybe not exactly,
but the words feel loving
and tender and true --
Well, maybe not to others,
but to me they really do.
And maybe I'll never have
those frilly things to say,
but Baby, whenever I think of you
I always think that way.

ON THE HEELS OF SUMMER

A breeze blew through from out of the north
and the nights cooled down to a chill;
then a two day rain showered on us
to cloud our weekend and to seal the deal.
And now you stand shivering in the water,
refusing to say what you know to be true,
that just as all good things
seem to find their ending on a whim,
today will be our very last swim of summer.

VIRTUAL FRIENDSHIP

Did you ever imagine
that there would come a day
when with just one finger,
in less than the blink of an eye,
and without
a second thought,
someone could
unfriend you?
Welcome
to the world
of antisocial media
where Callous
and his sister
Ridiculocity
reign supreme.

MY MUSE

Inspire me to create
by looking my way
with eyes that cannot hide
exquisite secrets that we keep.
Give me the smile
that ignites the fire
of a burning desire
to set free the art inside of me.
Your presence is my energy
and even when you're gone,
memories of you loving me
remain to serve
as my muse.

PRAYER OF SAINT SOMEBODY

Open my eyes that I may see
the lessons you are teaching me
along faraway sidewalks
or outside my own front door.
Help my feet that I may learn
on every good path or
at every wrong turn.
Set my mind correct as well
to know that the absence of mercy
creates a living hell --
not for those who live in need
but for those of us
too busy to feed, or to clothe,
or to love,
one another.
In return for these lessons,
I will open my hand
only and always at Your command
to give to others
what, in truth, belongs to You.

DRESSED FOR BATTLE

When you act like it didn't hurt,
the enemy feels challenged
to hit you again,
more forcefully this time
with more powerful ammunition.
So say aloud, "That hurt me"
and then assure the enemy
that you won't be hurting
for long.
On the outside
let the hurt honestly show
for just a moment
while on the inside
rejoice and give thanks
for endurance
against such wrong.
Evil will hit you
and it is going to sting,
but it cannot go in deep enough
to pierce the soul
if you will enter the battle
dressed in full armor
and guarding your heart
with a shield of faith.

HEART OF STONE

I collect heart shaped rocks
I've collected them for years
at the ocean's shoreline
from the forest's floor
in densely shaded woodlands
along the river banks
or while walking
on rusted railroad tracks
that no longer lead anywhere
Heart shaped rocks of
various sizes
never cease to amaze
with their form being the result
of gritty years
in sand and soil
being tossed about
from place to place
until refined by harsh winds
and hard rains
I bring them home
wash them off
admire their contour
love their nature
That's why I was not troubled
not even for a second
when you described yourself
as having a heart of stone
My life has been lived
in preparation for
someone just like you

DOWN - HOME POETRY

She writes verses
for those who sit on front porches,
for those sons
who read to their mother,
for those who copy down her words
to share with one another;
or who quote her prose
in a sweetly secret
letter to a lover.
If you prefer to read from lines
more abstract and artsy,
then her words are not for you;
they will not meet with your demand.
She writes for the common woman.
She writes for the common man.

WHEN WE BECOME ORPHANS

it's a different
kind
of ache,
it's a deep
and primal grief
that says
I need my momma.
I need to hear
her voice.
I need to hear
my name
being called
by the one
who said it
first.

NO DIRECTIONS NEEDED

All roads lead
to where I'm going
and I find satisfaction
in simply knowing
that the road I'm on
eventually
will lead precisely
to where I'll be
and somehow
that's enough for me
wandering aimlessly and free
devoid of particularity
with an abundance
of possibilities
traveling through life
with no direction home

ENCOMPASSED

On every road I travel
whether at home or abroad,
familiar or wilderness,
with certainty or when lost,
You have always been
my true north.

TRIBUTARY

He was fluid.
Flowing.
Love liquified.
And he alone
could quench
her thirst
just long enough
to leave her
wanting more.

HER TRAVEL ITINERARY

She says
I'll be fine
so long as I fall asleep
to the sound
inside my mind
of waves
rolling onto a sandy shore.
But on the night
that I rest in my bed
and no longer hear
the ocean
inside of my head,
I'll need to pack up
and hit the road.
She says
I'll stay put
so long as my mind
can see
tall golden aspens
dancing with the breeze;
as long as I can feel
icy-crisp mountain air,
I'll not need to go
anywhere.
I'll be still
until the images
fade
and then come early morning,
I'll be on my way
to the places that renew my spirit
and refresh my memory.

INDEBTED

He sent a note that read:
I only collect in a certain way
on a certain day --
on the thirty first of February.
Otherwise, and after that,
the debt is viewed
as paid in full.

She replied with a note in kind
which read:
In that case,
my heart will serve as collateral
and I will remain indebtedly yours
until the eleventeenth
of forever.

AFTER THE STORM

You took hold
of the hand
of the me
who only knew
how to be
a critic
a skeptic
untrusting
unsure
and with one
kind word
I heard
the beautiful sound
of possibility

KISMET

A buckeye in your pocket
A penny in your shoe
Lavender sprigs under your pillow
An arrowhead made of stone or bone
Salt over the left shoulder
A clover with four leaves
That rabbit's foot
kept in your treasure box
A pair of game winning socks
The sudden appearance of a rainbow
And then one day
somebody looks at you
in such a way
that from then on
you know
the true definition
of the word
lucky

FIRST WORLD DIETARY DILEMMA

You've tried being exclusively omnivore.
You've tried the route of the carnivore.
For one half of one weekend you swore
to become a meditative herbivore;
and so you recklessly downed
nine cups of green tea
with nearly a pound of clover honey.
And now you view your body
as a sugar coated carb-age can.
Perhaps it is time to consider
becoming the first ever
to proudly wear the title of
carb-avoid.

ETERNAL

Please don't tell me
that there comes a time
in every life
when a person is too old
for goofy smiles,
sweet dreams,
and long, slow kisses.
I need something to look forward to.

VOLVER   *

A wood frame house with a big front porch,
and blood red geraniums in terra cotta pots.
A home-sweet-home whose main entrance
is the torn screen door leading into the kitchen
where something is always simmering on the stove;
and in the garden waiting to be picked and peeled
and cut and cooked
is every tiny seed we planted,
now transformed into a harvest
to feed family and friends and anyone in need.
And the street is gravel and the street is dirt
and on the rare occasion that a car goes by,
it will travel at a crawl so as to not stir up dust
onto the linens on the line.
The big upstairs window
looks out at the live oak
that rustles in the wind at night, making music
as its branches brush against the screen.
And the best days end
whenever there was something in the mailbox --
a letter from family or from an old friend
that says I'm doing fine
but every time I think of you
I want to come back home.

* Volver is a Spanish verb meaning
to return or to go back.

ILLUSION & REALITY

Was I dreaming
or did we walk
through that field
of uncut wheat
and did your skin
look golden in the sun
and did you sing me to sleep
or was that just a dream
When I said that
I don't want this day to end
didn't you hold me close
and say I know what you mean
or was it all a dream
When I awoke to see you
looking at me
and looking as if
you'd just cried
and hearing you say
I want to die in your arms
and where ever is forever
I'll go there with you
was *that* just a dream
If these memories
are all that's left
of the us
that was me and you
then let me stay a while longer
inside of this bliss
I'm not ready to awaken
if all of this
was only a dream.

TRUTH OF THE MATTER

The enemy:
Someone whose life truly matters
but whose opinion – not so much

SWEET SURRENDER

O, my sins
to the breaking of my heart,
to the destruction of my being,
until my soul, once so tender,
became calloused and incapable
of discerning right from wrong,
until the light of righteousness
shined brighter than those wrongs
and cast strong beams of truth
to illuminate my weakness
so that under the weight
of a worn out calloused soul,
my heart broke
into countless pieces
only repairable
by the One
who first formed it.

PEACE TREATY

Same field
different soil
Whatever once was
rocky
thorny
wayside
unwilling to receive
the Word of Truth
has now become good
is now fertile again
Upon making amends
a wholesome wind
blew across this land
a strong
a mighty wind
Fresh air from heaven
changed the soil
and now anything
and everything
can grow here
in beauty
and in truth
and all that is
required of us
is to sow
peace

I FOUND GOD

Interesting expression,
considering the fact
that God was never lost.
It was you
who was in need
of being found.
When at last
you found God,
you, in all reality,
found yourself,
and standing there
at your side
was the Lord
your Creator,
your Father,
your God ~
where He'd been
all along.

SETTLED

Okay.
Me too.
We will.
I do.
There were no fireworks.
The earth did not shake.
Stars didn't explode
and fall to the ground.
Time did not stand still
She said okay,
Me too,
We will,
I do.

And now
she fills her days
reading the novels,
going to plays or
watching the movies,
memorizing the songs,
about fireworks,
stars falling from the sky,
and the kind of a love
that shakes the earth
until just for a moment
it feels to her
as if time is standing still.

VIRTUAL AFFECTION

There have been lovers
in recent history
whose sweet hearts
were separated
for months
and sometimes years
by dark days
of raging war.

There were lovers
just yesterday it seems
whose unions
were threatened
by religious divide
or by race,
ethnicity,
and social status.

We've come so far
since then.
You'd think we'd have
learned a thing or two.
But no, we see it
as the unquestionable end
before love has the chance
to begin

if he's not into texting
and she's not into face time.

REBOUNDING

Sometimes
for just a time
remove
from your
vocabulary
the wistful word
forever
and replace it
realistically
with
the notion of
for – now.

SECRET ASIAN MAN

Headed to the ladies room
to dry away her tears,
the man at the next table
tapped her on the elbow
then rose to whisper in her ear,
"If you will laugh when he
speaks to you that way,
he'll stop and think twice before he says
the things he has to say."

And so she did.
Upon returning to the table
and not waiting until he spoke,
she looked at him and laughed.
She laughed quietly to herself
and then she laughed out loud
until he knew that if he was looking
for someone to wail upon,
this girl would not do.

She stood to leave
and faced the table
where the wise, smiling man had been.
When she saw that he was gone,
she looked, and looked again
until she found him across the room
casually watching, preparing to advise
another soon-to-be-grateful
young damsel in distress.

POWERFUL AND BLUESY

The key of E speaks to me.
Just north of C,
down south of B.
The key of E says
start with me
and soon you'll see
we're meant to be.
So much less predictable
with a hint
of mystery,
so much more diverting
is life lived out
in the key of E

TWELVE SIBLINGS

The year gave birth to children ~
twelve, to be exact.

January, the firstborn,
perfectly chiseled like stone;
stern, staunch, and stoic,
dominating, somewhat dark,
the confident, motivated eldest child.

February ~ Flighty, unpredictable,
sentimental, always sweet,
proper and old fashioned,
surrendering ofttimes to melancholy.

March is forever apologetic
for sudden outbursts of uncontrollable
gusts that shatter and scatter
anything not tied down;
an otherwise shy traditionalist
and our wise historian.

And then

April and May, the twins ~
joyful and sunny, always optimistic
colorful pastels joined together,
forever hand in hand.

June, the middle child ~
a popular peacemaker, neither hot nor cold,
temperate, pleasant, never timid nor bold,
everybody's favorite.

July is the firecracker ~
exuberant and loud,
the life-is-a-party,
let's-stay-up-late,
let's-just-go-wild child.

August, ruddy, thick, and tall
calls himself the black sheep,
the unplanned addition,
the fiery, angry-for-no-reason child
who no one seems to understand
but whom everyone loves as best they can.

September, the maternal one, the family's core,
a tapestry made up of a little piece
of each month born before her
as well as the three that followed.

October will forever stay a child,
will forever wear layers upon layers
of color upon color,
flamboyantly living like royalty
without regard to constant warnings
issued by brother November.

November ~ The child with an old soul
who is incredibly attractive
despite forever wearing a frown;
never intending to stay around long,
November is the child you want to embrace
but he gets caught up on every north wind
and in the blink of an eye, is gone.

December ~ Everyone loves December
despite the tantrums of unpredictable weather.
December is the spiritual one, closest to the heart,
always insisting that every day
is cause for a celebration.
December is the baby,
the lovingly spoiled tail-end of the family,
decorated by the whims of eleven older siblings.

Each one of the twelve, unique in shape,
were masterfully designed
to fit together like a perfect puzzle
where each piece relies upon the other
to create the totality that makes them
the Family of the Year.

CREDO

Make the choice
to not live in the past
but rather to thrive
in the vastness
of each new day
new hour
new opportunity
to move forward
toward Joy

DUTCH TREAT

Here she comes now
with her bucket and her broom
and her wide eyes and her bangs.
And he wonders how it is
that over so many years
she's never grown old.
And he wonders how his vision,
once so sharp, so clear,
now determines
how he sees
this woman.
She winks at him
as she passes by
and is grateful to the core
that decades of living
have an aging effect
that cause him to see her
through a filtered lens of love.

FAIR WARNING

Raise the bar
Hold him to a higher standard
Expect more of him
than you did of them
And then
when he exceeds
your highest
expectations
don't be surprised
when the lack of an ovation
is by followed
by his departure
prompted by concern
that he now might view you
as the lesser
causing him
to seek
new challenges
to conquer
in order to maintain
his preference
for a level playing field

PASSIONATE KISSES

After all these years
she's grateful to say
that the only medication
she needs each day
is one small dose
of a blood pressure pill.
It's a pharmaceutical,
a chemical to control
the hypertension
that occurred when her heart
was called to attention
on the day of her very first
passionate kiss ~
That kiss that raised
her pulse and circulation
so far beyond
accepted limitations
that it has never since
been willing
to return to the norm.

ORIGINS

This could be the beginning
or this could be the end.
This could be
where you say goodbye,
or where new love begins.
You simply need to tell me
what's tumbling around
in your mind.
Is this just a spring time fling
or was that kiss the kind of thing
your seasoned heart has longed to find?

TERMINAL

If you insist
on cutting your life short
be sure that laughter
and shouts of joy
and singing
at the top of your lungs
and having cause
to say
Oh Wow
are regular
everyday experiences
on your way out of here

LONG DISTANCE

I'll always remember
that summertime
somewhere around two a.m.
when you phoned to say
you needed to hear
the sound of my voice again.
I remember your words
but most of all
I remember just after
hello,
how it seemed to me
that I could hear
a symphony in the silence
playing the unmistakable
music of your smile.

GOLDEN YEAR

In her golden year
he took her hand
and led her across
the chasm of alone
to a wide open world
born before winter
but later than spring
she'd memorized
his songs
before the fall

PAVLOVIAN

I'm willing to admit
that I do think about him now and then.
For instance, in the springtime --
we were good together in the spring
and he loved that time of year.
And then in summer,
of course I'm always
remembering us in summer,
laughing at each other
as we'd stay indoors to wait out
the high humidity.
Same for us in winter;
we'd sort of hibernate inside
to keep each other warm.
Oh yeah, I think about us
whenever it feels cold
in the wintertime.
And fall? O, Lord.
Every leaf, every color,
every breeze,
hc's there.
But other than that,
I can say for a fact
that he only enters my mind
from time to time.

ELEVEN FIFTY – NINE

It was one minute before midnight
when the telephone began to ring
on New Year's Eve.
I thought at first to answer
but didn't recognize the number
and so I let it ring.
I made the choice
that best suited me
in that moment
and even now.

I decided that I'd enjoy
spending the rest of winter
wondering who,
of everyone I've ever known,
telephoned
at the precise moment
when it was time
to give a kiss and loudly cheer
(or softly whisper in my ear)
Happy New Year.

TRANSPARITY

Your words of love
are round and full
beautiful ornaments
that you cleverly
and carefully
display
in my life.
The things you say
decorate my world
and give me cause
to celebrate.
But tell me this ~~
Is there a hook
on an ornament or two,
a fastening or a closure
that I can hang on to
to give me
some assurance
of your plans
or your hopes
for our future ~
something to give me
a reason to believe
that these
festive decorations
won't come down
at the end
of a short,
albeit beautiful,
season?

LONGFELLOW WANNABE

I look at what they're calling art
that sells for millions
and I know
like I know the backside of my hands
that I could splash some paint around
and be an esoteric enigmatic
really big artist in great demand
but my thing is really poetry;
yeah, I'm really really good with words
and people should stick
to what they know, right?

So give me a word, any word,
and watch me rhyme
or make a prose that really flows.
Yeah, gimme a word, anything.
No, not that one.
No, no -- not that.
Well, I guess right now
just isn't when writing's meant to be;
so hand me
the remote control.
Let's see what's on tv.

ISLA DEL SOL

There's a place I go,
Isla del Sol
on the Gulf of Mexico.
Where a street sign reads
'Watch For Sand On The Road'
(the only danger that they know).

If this land
America
was a fifty-room house,
then Isla del Sol
is what you'd see
when you'd look out
the south-side picture window.

And I believe it's what you'll see
on the day that your life
on earth is done.
When you go to live an eternity
in a place beyond the sun,
you'll enter a city
that bears a sweet resemblance
to Isla del Sol.

YOU SAID THERE WILL BE SUNSETS

but first let me finish this crossword
that I started earlier today
I need to fold this laundry pile and get it put away
and the dishes aren't going to wash themselves
I've got to watch the news to hear the weather report
and I still haven't checked the mail

You said there will be sunsets
and we'll watch them together
standing in the sand at Silver Strand
or at the Garden of The Gods or in the shade
of the choke cherry trees up in Jackson Hole
or while riding the trolley in Old Town San Diego

but you needed to finish something or other
that you'd started earlier in the day
and you needed to quickly return that call
so they'd know you were feeling okay
and so everyone would know that all is well

You said there will be sunsets
and you were right of course
I stand alone and watch them now
no longer something I might share with you
like a faithful friend sunsets come again each evening
and that's something that you cannot do
because death is a final sunset

WAITING ON THE FRONT PORCH

When my time on earth is over
and You come to take me home
to the Heaven you've prepared for me,
when you take me to my mansion,
Lord, could we stop along the way?
Could we stop at my mom's house
just for the morning,
or maybe into the rest of the day?

SUMMER IN THE SOUTH

I am very much a fan
of this laid-back kind of day.
I find that I'm inclined to recline
and to breathe in summertime
when the cotton white clouds
wear that wispy expression
while they play
hide and seek with the sun
as it turns to face
in my direction and shines
that 'Come on, I dare you' smile.

HIS PAST

The woods were dark,
coarse, and deeply textured
shades of jade
and emerald green
against endless hues in brown.
Unfamiliar strong branches
like fingers invited me in,
luring me forward,
hinting at longed-for embraces
with unspoken assurances
of relative safety at best
and of adventure for sure.
Encouraging me to employ
blind faith for the journey
combined with expectation
that somewhere along the way
there'd be a clearing
and the light of day
streaming downward,
breaking the heavy canopy of
shade and shadow,
I entered what was, in all reality,
the ancient forest of a soul
entangled in a quixotic,
exotic, and vexingly neurotic
jungle
where many had entered
before me,
none of whom escaped.

HOWDY MISS MERTIE

Just because you smell the smell
of berry cobbler 'round her kitchen window,
does not mean she's home to answer the call
should you try to phone.

And just because the towels and sheets
are hanging on the line,
does not mean she has the time
to sit around and shoot the breeze.

When you walk by and see her
in the garden pulling weeds,
she's not out there to hear the latest gossip.
She's busy doin' busy kinds of things.

And when you see her silhouette
rocking by the front room window,
don't figure that she's relaxing or doing
what lazy people do at the end of *their* day.

She's sittin' and she's wonderin'
why she feels so all alone
while everyone else is sitting at home
laughing and loving on each other.

Miss Mertie is so doggone lonely
at the close of every day
and for the life of her
she cannot begin to figure out why.

SOLDIER'S BRIDE

The prospect of no return
has precious little to do
with the fact
that for now and forever
I will wait for you
I'll post watch at the window
I'll listen
through the night
because that's what my heart
has been trained to do
for now and for always
I will wait for you

IN THE SHADOW OF THE MOON

Please don't waste your time
with what ifs
or how come.
Instead,
when you remember me,
remind your heart
that at least
we had September.

AANBIDDEN   *

God is praised in different ways.
For some, with loud cheers;
for others, with reverent tears.
Voices that praise the Ancient of Days
can raise the roof or shake the tents
or illuminate a darkened world
in the beautiful solitude of holy silence.

* The Dutch word for worship is aanbidden

OUTCOME: IRRELEVANT

I stayed in my own lane
and obeyed all the rules
never broke the law
paid my bills on time
arrived ten minutes early
always playing it safe
never testing fate
never taking chances
never gambling on life
unwilling to cast
my fortune to the wind
until I met you
And then
blind faith guided me
into your arms
where it felt right
to be reckless
and to abandon common sense
It was as if
for all my life
I'd been saving up
watching and waiting
for that one frivolous
serendipitous
split-second choice
to either keep on keeping on
or to take a chance
on love
Ignoring the likely outcome
what else could I do
I'm grateful to this day
that I took a chance on You

DEDICATION

Providing the body
while hiding the soul
keeping it buried
so deep
that even the length
of a warrior's sword
cannot begin to breach
the cords that form this bond
and its secrets that we keep
such as this abiding truth
that I only write for you
While others will recite
rewrite
and put my words
into public view
the truth remains
to the end of time
I only wrote for you
My words are just for you

WHEN YOU LOVE A BOY

O, the crazy things you'll do
when you love a boy.
You'll hurry home so he can phone
after you spent all day
side-by-side in every class
at the desk across from his.
You'll help him with his essay
because he helps you with the math
and you'll write his name on anything
a couple dozen times
when you love a boy.
You'll do all these things and more
in exchange for the sound of his voice
declaring, "We're going together"
or "I am yours."
When you love a boy,
you'll up and move away from home
to dwell in unknown lands beside him,
always there to let him know
that you're the one who wants
to wake him up each morning
and at the ending of his day,
to stay up late awaiting
the sound of his key in the door
that announces that your beloved

has returned to you once more.
And when his body gives your body
the gift of a son,
O, the crazy things you'll do
when you love a boy.
You'll endure the stinkiness
and the constant mess
and the bedside nursing and his forgetfulness.
For the love of your boy,
you'll fight for him as you'd defend no other
in exchange for the sound of
his voice calling out
Mother, Mother. Mother !

TURN AND FACE THE WIND

It will always seem easier
to walk through life
with the wind at your back
to be pushed along
by a gust that is gentle
or a force that is strong

You are a part of the majority
if you traverse your path
with the wind at your back
moving in pace
with this world's demands
with those who
like you grew up believing
that to be propelled forward
in whatever way the wind may blow
is the chosen way
we all must go

No

Some winds come loudly
with the sound of disappointment
short term gladness
daily chaos
occasional madness
Why continue to be blown
through life
like just another fallen leaf

Why not take a closer look
at the you who was created

different than them
different than me
Look at how strong
you have the potential to be

Those strong winds behind you
contain nothing you can't face
Wind was not created
to move you
from place to place
Remember who you are
Remember your great worth
You were destined for excellence
since the day of your birth
Now turn and face the wind

BOOKS BY THIS AUTHOR:

Turn And Face The Wind
(poetry)

In Her Own Native Tongue
(poetry)

Song Of Bethlehem
(historical fiction)

Saint Somebody
(memoir)

These books are available through Amazon and other major book sellers or may be purchased directly from the author at:

Teresa Prins Wood
Post Office Box 1293
Sand Springs, Oklahoma
74063

For more information, visit her web site:
www.teresaprinswood.com

100% of the profits Teresa receives for sales of her books is used to purchase necessities for the homeless, for homeless shelters, and for non profit safe houses and shelters that provide residency to survivors of abuse.

Made in the USA
Coppell, TX
21 March 2022

75317839R00111